THE _____

THE WISDOM OF
THE PROPHETS

Compiled by Philip Law
Introduced by Donald Coggan

LION
Giftlines

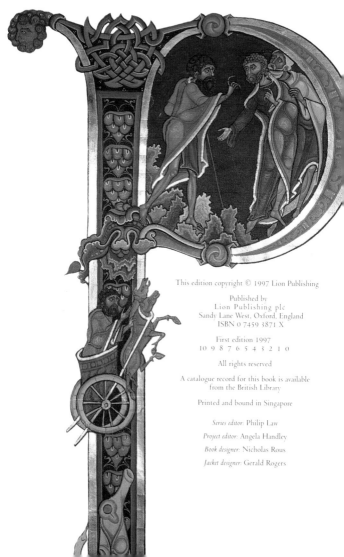

This edition copyright © 1997 Lion Publishing

Published by
Lion Publishing plc
Sandy Lane West, Oxford, England
ISBN 0 7459 3871 X

First edition 1997
10 9 8 7 6 5 4 3 2 1 0

A catalogue record for this book is available
from the British Library

Printed and bound in Singapore

Series editor: Philip Law

Project editor: Angela Handley

Book designer: Nicholas Rous

Jacket designer: Gerald Rogers

CONTENTS

INTRODUCTION

The Old Testament is a small library. Within its thirty-nine books are to be found history and legend, poetry and prose, drama and devotion.

Phrases from these books have woven themselves into the texture of English language and literature, through the influence of such men as William Tyndale and through the labours of the translators of the King James Version of 1611.

The writings of the New Testament cannot be understood without some appreciation of the Old Testament books. Among these books, those of the prophets stand out for their spiritual and moral forthrightness. We neglect them at our peril, for the truths they present are timeless and, many of us would add, God-given. One has only to glance at the extracts provided by this book to see their permanent value – Isaiah's vision of the holiness of God (5), Elijah's experience of God in the 'sound of sheer silence' (4), the rugged insistence of Zechariah on justice and compassion (15), the passion of the suffering servant of Isaiah pointing us to the person of Christ (16).

The Wisdom of the Prophets is the title of this book. Wisdom demands attention on the part of those who are confronted by it. There are at least two ways in which these extracts can be viewed. One is to view them as daily meditations. Each day for a month let one extract be at the centre of your thinking. Read it at the beginning of the day, let it recur to your mind during the course of the day, ponder it at the end of the day. In this way, the wisdom of the prophets might well become your own.

These extracts may also be viewed as an invitation to further exploration in the rich field of Hebrew prophecy. After all, they are only extracts, and are best seen in the context of Hebrew prophecy as a whole.

DONALD COGGAN

PROLOGUE

I

He has told you, O mortal, what is good;
and what does the Lord require of you
but to do justice, and to love kindness,
and to walk humbly with your God?

Micah 6:8

REVELATIONS OF THE SPIRIT

2

The Lord is in his holy temple:
let all the earth keep silence before him.

Habakkuk 2:20

3

The Name of God

Now Moses was tending the flock of Jethro his
father-in-law, the priest of Midian, and he led
the flock to the far side of the desert and came
to Horeb, the mountain of God. There the
angel of the Lord appeared to him in flames of
fire from within a bush. Moses saw that though
the bush was on fire it did not burn up. So
Moses thought, 'I will go over and see this
strange sight – why the bush does not burn up.'

When the Lord saw that he had gone over
to look, God called to him from within the
bush, 'Moses! Moses!'

And Moses said, 'Here I am.'

'Do not come any closer,' God said. 'Take
off your sandals, for the place where you are
standing is holy ground'… At this, Moses hid
his face, because he was afraid to look at God.

The Lord said, 'I have indeed seen the
misery of my people in Egypt. I have heard
them crying out because of their slave drivers,

and I am concerned about their suffering... So now, go. I am sending you to Pharaoh to bring my people the Israelites out of Egypt...'

Moses said to God, 'Suppose I go to the Israelites and say to them, "The God of your fathers has sent me to you," and they ask me, "What is his name?" Then what shall I tell them?'

God said to Moses, 'I AM WHO I AM. This is what you are to say to the Israelites: "I AM has sent me to you."'

Exodus 3:1–8, 10, 13–14

THE SOUND OF SILENCE

[Elijah] went a day's journey into the wilderness, and came and sat down under a solitary broom tree. He asked that he might die: 'It is enough; now, O Lord, take away my life, for I am no better than my ancestors.' Then he lay down under the broom tree and fell asleep. Suddenly an angel touched him and said to him, 'Get up and eat.' He looked, and there at his head was a cake baked on hot stones, and a jar of water. He ate and drank, and lay down again. The angel of the Lord came a second time, touched him, and said, 'Get up and eat, otherwise the journey will be too much for you.' He got up, and ate and drank; then he went in the strength of that food for forty days and forty nights to Horeb the mount of God. At that place he came to a cave, and spent the night there.

Then the word of the Lord came to him, saying, 'What are you doing here, Elijah?'

He answered, 'I have been very zealous for the Lord, the God of hosts; for the Israelites have forsaken your covenant, thrown down your altars, and killed your prophets with the sword. I alone am left, and they are seeking my life, to take it away.'

He said, 'Go out and stand on the mountain before the Lord, for the Lord is about to pass by.' Now there was a great wind, so strong that it was splitting mountains and breaking rocks in pieces before the Lord, but the Lord was not in the wind; and after the wind an earthquake, but the Lord was not in the earthquake; and after the earthquake a fire, but the Lord was not in the fire; and after the fire a sound of sheer silence. When Elijah heard it, he wrapped his face in his mantle and went out...

1 Kings 19:4–13

THE KING OF HEAVEN

In the year that King Uzziah died I saw the
Lord seated on a throne, high and exalted,
and the skirt of his robe filled the temple.
Seraphim were in attendance on him. Each had
six wings: with one pair of wings they covered
their faces and with another their bodies, and
with the third pair they flew. They were calling
to one another,

> Holy, holy, holy is the Lord of Hosts:
> the whole earth is full of his glory.

As each called, the threshold shook to its
foundations at the sound, while the house
began to fill with clouds of smoke. Then I said,

> Woe is me! I am doomed,
> for my own eyes have seen the King,
>   the Lord of Hosts,
> I, a man of unclean lips,
> I, who dwell among a people of unclean lips.

One of the seraphim flew to me, carrying in
his hand a glowing coal which he had taken
from the altar with a pair of tongs. He
touched my mouth with it and said,

This has touched your lips;
now your iniquity is removed
and your sin is wiped out.

Isaiah 6:1–7

THE CHARIOT OF GOD

On the fifth day of the fourth month in the thirtieth year, while I was among the exiles by the river Kebar, the heavens were opened and I saw visions from God...

In my vision I saw a storm-wind coming from the north, a vast cloud with flashes of fire and brilliant light about it; and within was a radiance like brass, glowing in the heart of the flames. In the fire was the likeness of four living creatures in human form. Each had four faces and each four wings... all four had a human face and a lion's face on the right, on the left the face of an ox and the face of an eagle...

As I looked at the living creatures, I saw wheels on the ground, one beside each of the four. The wheels sparkled like topaz, and they were all alike: in form and working they were like a wheel inside a wheel, and when they moved in any of the four directions they never swerved from their course. I saw that they had rims, and the rims were covered with eyes all around…

I heard, too, the noise of their wings; when they moved it was like the noise of a mighty torrent or a thunderclap, like the noise of a crowd or an armed camp; when they halted their wings dropped. A voice was heard from above the vault over their heads, as they halted with drooping wings.

Above the vault over their heads there appeared, as it were, a sapphire in the shape of a throne, and exalted on the throne a form in human likeness. From his waist upwards I saw what might have been brass glowing like fire in a furnace; and from his waist downwards I saw what looked like fire. Radiance encircled him. Like a rainbow in the clouds after the rain was the sight of that encircling radiance; it was like the appearance of the glory of the Lord.

Ezekiel 1:1, 4–6, 10, 15–18, 24–28a

THE ANCIENT OF DAYS

I beheld till the thrones were cast down, and the Ancient of days did sit, whose garment was white as snow, and the hair of his head like the pure wool: his throne was like the fiery flame, and his wheels as burning fire. A fiery stream issued and came forth from before him: thousand thousands ministered unto him, and ten thousand times ten thousand stood before him: the judgment was set, and the books were opened...

I saw in the night visions, and, behold, one like the Son of man came with the clouds of heaven, and came to the Ancient of days, and they brought him near before him. And there was given him dominion, and glory, and a kingdom, that all people, nations, and languages, should serve him: his dominion is an everlasting dominion, which shall not pass away, and his kingdom that which shall not be destroyed.

Daniel 7:9–10, 13–14

VOICES IN THE WILDERNESS

8

Let justice roll on like a river,
righteousness like a never-failing stream!

Amos 5:24

Prepare the Way

The voice of him that crieth in the wilderness,
Prepare ye the way of the Lord,
make straight in the desert
a highway for our God.
Every valley shall be exalted,
and every mountain and hill shall be made low:
and the crooked shall be made straight,
and the rough places plain:
And the glory of the Lord shall be revealed,
and all flesh shall see it together…
The voice said, Cry.
And he said, What shall I cry?
All flesh is grass,
and all the goodliness thereof is as the flower
    of the field…
The grass withereth, the flower fadeth:
but the word of our God shall stand for ever.

Isaiah 40:6, 8

The Power of God

Who hath measured the waters in the hollow
    of his hand,
and meted out heaven with the span,
and comprehended the dust of the earth in
    a measure,
and weighed the mountains in scales,
and the hills in a balance?
Who hath directed the Spirit of the Lord,
or being his counsellor hath taught him?
With whom took he counsel,
and who instructed him,
and taught him in the path of judgment,
and taught him knowledge,
and shewed to him the way of understanding?...
It is he that sitteth upon the circle of the earth,
and the inhabitants thereof are as grasshoppers;
that stretcheth out the heavens as a curtain,
and spreadeth them out as a tent to dwell in.

Isaiah 40:12–14, 22

THE JUDGMENT OF GOD

The heart is devious above all else;
it is perverse —
who can understand it?
I the Lord test the mind
and search the heart,
to give to all according to their ways,
according to the fruit of their doings.

Jeremiah 17:9–10

THE TRANSCENDENCE OF GOD

Why do you spend your money for that which is
    not bread,
and your labour for that which does not satisfy?
Listen carefully to me, and eat what is good,
and delight yourselves in rich food.
Incline your ear, and come to me;
listen, so that you may live...

Seek the Lord while he may be found,
call upon him while he is near;
let the wicked forsake their way,
and the unrighteous their thoughts;
let them return to the Lord, that he may have
    mercy on them,
and to our God, for he will abundantly pardon.
For my thoughts are not your thoughts,
nor are your ways my ways, says the Lord.
For as the heavens are higher than the earth,
so are my ways higher than your ways
and my thoughts than your thoughts.

Isaiah 55:2–3a, 6–9

THE WISDOM OF GOD

Surely there is a mine for silver,
and a place for gold to be refined.
Iron is taken out of the earth,
and copper is smelted from ore.
Miners put an end to darkness,
and search out to the farthest bound
the ore in gloom and deep darkness…

But where shall wisdom be found?
And where is the place of understanding?
Mortals do not know the way to it,
and it is not found in the land of the living.
The deep says, 'It is not in me,'
and the sea says, 'It is not with me.'
It cannot be bought for gold,
and silver cannot be weighed out as its price.
It cannot be valued in the gold of Ophir,
in precious onyx or sapphire.
Gold and glass cannot equal it,
nor can it be exchanged for jewels of fine gold…

Where then does wisdom come from?
And where is the place of understanding?

God understands the way to it,
and he knows its place.
For he looks to the ends of the earth,
and sees everything under the heavens.
When he gave to the wind its weight,
and apportioned out the waters by measure;
when he made a decree for the rain,
and a way for the thunderbolt;
then he saw it and declared it;
he established it, and searched it out.
And he said to humankind,
'Truly, the fear of the Lord, that is wisdom;
and to depart from evil is understanding.'

Job 28:1–3, 12–17, 20, 23–28

The Knowledge of God

Thus says the Lord: Do not let the wise boast in their wisdom, do not let the mighty boast in their might, do not let the wealthy boast in their wealth; but let those who boast boast in this, that they understand and know me, that I am the Lord; I act with steadfast love, justice, and righteousness in the earth, for in these things I delight, says the Lord.

Jeremiah 9:23–24

THE JUSTICE OF GOD

Thus speaketh the Lord of hosts, saying,
Execute true judgment, and shew mercy and
compassions every man to his brother: And
oppress not the widow, nor the fatherless,
the stranger, nor the poor; and let none of you
imagine evil against his brother in your heart.

Zechariah 7:9–10

GOD'S SUFFERING SERVANT

He was despised and rejected by men;
a man of sorrows, and acquainted with grief;
and as one from whom men hide their faces
he was despised, and we esteemed him not.

Surely he has borne our griefs
and carried our sorrows;
yet we esteemed him stricken,
smitten by God, and afflicted.
But he was wounded for our transgressions,
he was bruised for our iniquities;
upon him was the chastisement
that made us whole,
and with his stripes we are healed.
All we like sheep have gone astray;
we have turned every one to his own way;
and the Lord has laid on him
the iniquity of us all.

Isaiah 53:3–6

VISIONS OF PEACE

Of those who are sleeping in the Land
of Dust, many will awaken, some to
everlasting life, some to shame and
everlasting disgrace. Those who are wise
will shine as brightly as the expanse of the
heavens, and those who have instructed
many in uprightness, as bright as stars
for all eternity.

Daniel 12:2–3

No Peace for the Wicked

For thus says the high and lofty One
who inhabits eternity, whose name is Holy:
'I dwell in the high and holy place,
and also with him who is of a contrite and
humble spirit,
to revive the spirit of the humble,
and to revive the heart of the contrite.
For I will not contend for ever,
nor will I always be angry;
for from me proceeds the spirit,
and I have made the breath of life...
Peace, peace, to the far and to the near,
says the Lord;
and I will heal him.
But the wicked are like the tossing sea;
for it cannot rest,
and its waters toss up mire and dirt.
There is no peace, says my God, for the wicked.'

Isaiah 57:15–16, 19–21

NO MORE WAR

But in the last days it shall come to pass,
that the mountain of the house of the Lord
shall be established in the top of the mountains,
and it shall be exalted above the hills;
and people shall flow unto it.
And many nations shall come, and say,
Come, and let us go up to the mountain of
   the Lord,
and to the house of the God of Jacob;
and he will teach us of his ways,
and we will walk in his paths:
for the law shall go forth of Zion,
and the word of the Lord from Jerusalem.
And he shall judge among many people,
and rebuke strong nations afar off;
and they shall beat their swords into plowshares,
and their spears into pruninghooks:
nation shall not lift up a sword against nation,
neither shall they learn war any more.

Micah 4:1–3

All Shall be Well

The Spirit of the Lord God is upon me;
because the Lord hath anointed me
to preach good tidings unto the meek;
he hath sent me to bind up the brokenhearted,
to proclaim liberty to the captives,
and the opening of the prison to them that
    are bound;
To proclaim the acceptable year of the Lord,
and the day of vengeance of our God;
to comfort all that mourn;
To appoint unto them that mourn in Zion,
to give unto them beauty for ashes,
the oil of joy for mourning,
the garment of praise for the spirit of heaviness;
that they might be called trees of righteousness,
the planting of the Lord,
that he might be glorified.

Isaiah 61:1–2

THE WAY OF HOLINESS

The wilderness and the solitary place shall be
glad… and the desert shall rejoice, and
blossom as the rose.

Then the eyes of the blind shall be opened,
and the ears of the deaf shall be unstopped.
Then shall the lame man leap as an hart,
and the tongue of the dumb sing:
for in the wilderness shall waters break out,
and streams in the desert…
And an highway shall be there, and a way,
and it shall be called the way of holiness…
And the ransomed of the Lord shall return,
and come to Zion with songs and everlasting
joy upon their heads:
they shall obtain joy and gladness,
and sorrow and sighing shall flee away.

Isaiah 35:1, 5–6, 8a, 10

THE NEW CREATION

See, I am creating new heavens and a new
earth! The past will no more be remembered
nor will it ever come to mind…
No child there will ever again
die in infancy, no old man fail
to live out his span of life. He
who dies at a hundred is just
a youth, and if he does not
attain a hundred he is thought
accursed! My people will build
houses and live in them, plant
vineyards and eat their fruit;
they will not build for others to live in or
plant for others to eat. They will be as long-
lived as a tree, and my chosen ones will enjoy
the fruit of their labour.

Isaiah 65:17, 20–22

THE PEACEABLE KINGDOM

Then the wolf will live with the lamb,
and the leopard lie down with the kid;
the calf and the young lion will feed together,
with a little child to tend them.
The cow and the bear will be friends,
and their young will lie down together;
and the lion will eat straw like cattle.
The infant will play over the cobra's hole,
and the young child dance over the viper's nest.
There will be neither hurt nor harm in all my
    holy mountain;
for the land will be filled with the knowledge
    of the Lord,
as the waters cover the sea.

Isaiah 11:6–9

PRAYERS OF DOUBT AND TRUST

24

O Lord, how long shall I cry for help,
  and thou wilt not hear?
Or cry to thee 'Violence!'
  and thou wilt not save?
Why dost thou make me see wrongs
  and look upon trouble?

Habakkuk 1:2–3

THE HUMAN CONDITION

Man that is born of a woman is of few days and full of trouble. He cometh forth like a flower, and is cut down: he fleeth also as a shadow, and continueth not...

For there is hope of a tree, if it be cut down, that it will sprout again, and that the tender branch thereof will not cease. Though the root thereof wax old in the earth, and the stock thereof die in the ground; Yet through the scent of water it will bud, and bring forth boughs like a plant.

But man dieth, and wasteth away: yea, man giveth up the ghost, and where is he? As the waters fail from the sea, and the flood decayeth and drieth up: So man lieth down, and riseth not: till the heavens be no more, they shall not awake, nor be raised out of their sleep.

O that thou wouldest hide me in the grave, that thou wouldest keep me secret, until thy wrath be past, that thou wouldest appoint me a set time, and remember me! If a man die, shall he live again? all the days of my appointed time will I wait, till my change come. Thou shalt call, and I will answer thee: thou wilt have a desire to the work of thine hands.

Job 14:1–2, 7–15

SUFFERING AND HOPE

It is of the Lord's mercies that we are not
    consumed,
because his compassions fail not.
They are new every morning:
great is thy faithfulness.
The Lord is my portion, saith my soul;
therefore will I hope in him.
The Lord is good unto them that wait for him,
to the soul that seeketh him...
For the Lord will not cast off for ever:
But though he cause grief, yet will he have
    compassion according to the multitude
    of his mercies.
For he doth not afflict willingly
nor grieve the children of men.

Lamentations 3:22–25, 31–33

THE LORD WILL SAVE

I thought that in the prime of life
I was going to the world of the dead,
Never to live out my life…
My life was cut off and ended,
Like a tent that is taken down,
Like cloth that is cut from a loom…
My voice was thin and weak,
And I moaned like a dove.
My eyes grew tired from looking to heaven.
Lord, rescue me from all this trouble.
What can I say? The Lord has done this.
My heart is bitter, and I cannot sleep.
Lord, I will live for you, for you alone;
Heal me and let me live.
My bitterness will turn into peace…
No one in the world of the dead can praise you;
The dead cannot trust in your faithfulness.
It is the living who praise you,
As I praise you now.

Isaiah 38:10, 12, 14–19

THE LORD WILL COMFORT

O Lord, you are my God;
I will exalt you, I will praise your name;
for you have done wonderful things,
plans formed of old, faithful and sure…
For you have been a refuge to the poor,
a refuge to the needy in their distress,
a shelter from the rainstorm and a shade
    from the heat.
When the blast of the ruthless was like
    a winter rainstorm,
the noise of aliens like heat in a dry place,
you subdued the heat with the shade of clouds;
the song of the ruthless was stilled.

On this mountain the Lord of hosts
will make for all peoples
a feast of rich food,
a feast of well-matured wines,
of rich food filled with marrow,
of well-matured wines strained clear.

And he will destroy
on this mountain
the shroud that
is cast over all
peoples, the sheet
that is spread over
all nations; he will
swallow up death
for ever.

Then the Lord
God will wipe away
the tears from all faces, and the disgrace of his
people he will take away from all the earth, for
the Lord has spoken.

Isaiah 25:1, 4–8

THE LORD WILL FORGIVE

There is no other god like you, O Lord; you forgive the sins of your people… You do not stay angry for ever, but you take pleasure in showing us your constant love. You will be merciful to us once again. You will trample our sins underfoot and send them to the bottom of the sea!

Micah 7:18–19

EPILOGUE

30

THE TEN COMMANDMENTS

Thou shalt have no other gods before me.
Thou shalt not make… any graven image…
Thou shalt not take the name of the Lord
thy God in vain…
Remember the sabbath day, to keep it holy…
Honour thy father and thy mother…
Thou shalt not kill.
Thou shalt not commit adultery.
Thou shalt not steal.
Thou shalt not bear false witness…
Thou shalt not covet any thing that is
thy neighbour's.

Exodus 20:3–4, 7–8, 12–17

Text Acknowledgments

Extracts 1, 4, 11, 12, 13, 14 and 28 are taken from the New Revised Standard Version of the Bible, copyright © 1989 by the Division of Christian Education of the National Council of Churches of Christ in the USA.

Extracts 2, 7, 9, 10, 15, 19, 20, 21, 25, 26 and 30 are taken from the Authorised Version of the Bible (The King James Bible), the rights of which are vested in the Crown, are reproduced by permission of the Crown's Patentee, Cambridge University Press.

Extracts 3 and 8 are taken from the HOLY BIBLE, NEW INTERNATIONAL VERSION. Copyright © 1973, 1978, 1984 by International Bible Society. Used by permission of Hodder and Stoughton Ltd. All rights reserved. 'NIV' is a registered trademark of International Bible Society. UK trademark number 1448790.

Extracts 5, 6, 22 and 23 are taken from the Revised English Bible © 1989 by permission of Oxford and Cambridge University Presses.

Extracts 16, 18 and 24 are taken from the Revised Standard Version of the Bible, copyright © 1946, 1952, 1971 by the Division of Christian Education of the Churches of Christ in the USA.

Extract 17 is taken from the New Jerusalem Bible © 1985 by Darton, Longman and Todd Ltd and Doubleday and Company, Inc.

Extracts 27 and 29 are taken from the *Good News Bible* published by the Bible Societies/HarperCollins Publishers Ltd UK © American Bible Society, 1966, 1971,1976, 1992.

Picture Acknowledgments

Page 1 (Jonah brought up by the whale, window in Canterbury Cathedral, 13th century), page 4 (Elijah and the messengers of Ahaziah, and Elijah in the fiery chariot, Winchester Bible, folio 120), page 7 (Daniel in the lion's den, window in St Etienne, Mulhouse, 14th century), page 9 (Jeremiah, mural in the Church of the Saviour, Paleochorio, Cyprus, Philip Goul, 15th century), pages 11, 21, 31 and 39 (Habakkuk, Gideon, Daniel and Elijah, respectively, one of twelve prophets in the dome of the Church of Panagia Tou Arakou, Lagondera, Cyprus, 1192), page 24 (Jeremiah holding a scroll, mosaic in San Vitale, Ravenna, 6th century), page 29 (Zaccharias, Daphni, Greece, 11th century), page 36 (Isaiah, detail from Jesse window in St Mary's Church, Shrewsbury), page 45 (Isaiah, detail from east window, Exeter Cathedral, 14th century) all reproduced courtesy of Sonia Halliday.

Pages 2–3 (Elijah taken up in a chariot of fire, painting by Giovanni Battista Piazzetta, 1683–1754) reproduced courtesy of the Samuel H. Kress Collection, National Gallery of Art, Washington DC, USA.

Page 13 (Moses at the burning bush, window in Malvern Priory) reproduced courtesy of Ffotograff.

Artwork

Pages 5 and 6, 17, 28, 41 and 46 by Amanda Barlow.